Purple

Cat

Waves

Bubbles

Fruit

Peacock

Sunrise

Blue

Mountaintop

Puddles

Reflection

Closet

Rope

Springtime

Ferns

Cottage

Forest

Horses

Goggles

Prince

Love

Music

Flower

Candle

Cave

Loom

Guitar

Map

Lions

Green

Hand

Bookshelf

Moon

Snowy

Banana

Eye

Octopus

Baby

Money

Grass

Pattern

Frog

Lamp

Driftwood

Clouds

Perspective

Rose

Silk

Crayon

Palm

Yellow

Piano

Checkerboard

Quail

Warm

Fire

Ice

Pool

Dissolve

Butter

Jello

Pancakes

Worm

Can

Lemon

Sheep

Run

Wash

Ink

Slow

Orchid

Melon

Zebra

Noodles

Mug

Stone

Crystal

Handle

Mom

Cry

Dog

Red

Volcano

Party

Skeleton

Angel

Cake

Rebirth

Airplane

Fear

Knife

Target

Man

Earth

Dinosaur

Pencil

Suitcase

Dragon

Treasure

Bun

Milk

www.ingramcontent.com/pod-product-compliance
Lightning Source LLC
Chambersburg PA
CBHW070427220526
45466CB00004B/1576